Ephesians

Kevin Archer

Copyright 2016 by Kevin Archer.
The book author retains sole copyright to
his contributions to this book.
Published 2016.
Printed in the United States of America.

All rights reserved.

No portion of this book may be reproduced, stored in a retrieval system, or transmitted in any form or by any means – electronic, mechanical, photocopy, recording, scanning, or other – except for brief quotations in critical reviews or articles, without the prior written permission of the author.

ISBN 978-1-946234-04-9

Front cover design by Mark Gauthier.

This book was published by BookCrafters,
Parker, Colorado.
bookcrafterscolorado@gmail.com

This book may be ordered from
www.bookcrafters.net and other online bookstores.

Foreword

Thank you for selecting this volume of the Expository series. These volumes are the contribution of various Apostolic writers. Their biography is on the back cover. The publishers of the Expository series would like to extend a thank you for helping us get this valuable material into the hands of readers.

The desire is that people would read the scriptures and be blessed. These commentary works, or works of Expository subjects, will give insight to, and further the understanding of the readers.

Each of these authors hold the values of the original Apostles of Jesus Christ. These writers want to hold to the values expostulated in the New Testament by Jesus and his disciples. Each of them ascribe to the concept offered by the Apostle John, "I have no greater joy than to hear that my children walk in truth."

Truth has been passed down through generations and has survived critics and doubters. Truth will prevail and ultimately triumph.

These writings are our contribution to the river of written truth that has flowed down through the ages.

Read and be blessed.

Kenneth Bow

Introduction

This epistle, by the pen of the Apostle Paul, was written in Rome during his imprisonment there, sometime around the years of 60-62 AD. His claim to authorship was expressly stated in chapter 1:1 "Paul, an apostle of Jesus Christ by the will of God, to the saints and to the faithful." and also in chapter 3:1 where he states: "I Paul, the prisoner of Jesus Christ for you Gentiles,"

Recipients:

It most likely was not just written exclusively to the local church at Ephesus. Here are a few facts that support this reasoning: 1) The author omits any personal greetings or salutations. 2) The word "church" used throughout it defines as "church universal." 3) He doesn't address any specific local church problem. 4) Chapter 3:2 would indicate that not all of the recipients had actually met him but only had heard of him. It appears to be a safe assumption that it was written to more than just one specific assembly found only in the city of Ephesus. It rather was probably passed through out all of the surrounding churches in the form of a circular letter.

The need addressed:

Due to the proclivity of converted Jewish Christians to be an exclusive and separated people to themselves, and newly converted Gentile Christians ignorance of all such customs, it was necessary for the Apostle to write this epistle centered around the theme of "Unity." There was a clashing of two cultures that would need to be blended together into the "Culture of Christ."

Theme: Unity of the Church:

If one scripture could sum up the entirety of this epistle, it would aptly be: 4:13 Till we all come in the unity of the faith, and of the knowledge of the Son of God, unto a perfect man, unto the measure of the stature of the fullness of Christ:

Paul lays out the outline for unity throughout this writing with words like "Together" In God's kingdom, according to Eph. 1:10 1) He "gathers together in one all things in Christ," In Eph. 2:5 He "hath quickened us together with Christ" In Eph. 2:6 He "hath raised us up together," and He "made us sit together in heavenly places" Finally in Eph. 2:22 We are builded together for an habitation of God through the Spirit.

He also uses the word "One" which indicates unity. In chapter 2:15...to make in himself of twain ONE new man... In chapter 2:16 "he reconciled both Jew and Gentile believers unto God in ONE body by the cross, in chapter 2:18 the writer states that both nationalities have access to the Father by ONE Spirit. Chapter 4:4-6 says that the believer has ONE hope that belongs to his or her calling, ONE Lord, ONE faith, ONE baptism, ONE God and Father of all.

A child of God has all of these spiritual blessings by virtue of the fact that they are chosen by God in Him (Christ). They that are IN HIM have unity with Christ and also unity with one another. As the psalmist wrote, in Psa. 133:1 ¶ Behold, how good and how pleasant it is for brethren to dwell together in unity!

Chapter 1

1.1-3 Paul, an apostle of Jesus Christ by the will of God, to the saints which are at Ephesus, and to the faithful in Christ Jesus: 2 Grace be to you, and peace, from God our Father, and from the Lord Jesus Christ. 3 Blessed be the God and Father of our Lord Jesus Christ, who hath blessed us with all spiritual blessings in heavenly places in Christ:

1.1-3 Paul's salutation to the saints of God identified him as an Apostle of Jesus Christ (one that is a guarantor of true Christian doctrine and appropriate instructor on all Christian conduct.) His Apostleship wasn't the result of mankind's choice but because it was "by the Will of God." It should then be understood that his message was sent by the highest of authority: it was sent from God and should be received and obeyed.

"Blessed be" the God and Father of our Lord Jesus Christ, was a use of traditional language that was used in Old testament times, now being used by Paul, and other New Testament writers, identifying Jesus as the recipient of all such blessings rather than the use of the phrase "God of Israel" as was done in the Old Testament. **"Heavenly places in Christ"** is a reference to a spiritual dimension in Christ that a believer has been blessed to exist in while living in this present world. The believer's life is lived in dimension of overlap between this present world and that, which is to come.

1.4-6 According as he hath chosen us in him before the foundation of the world, that we should be holy and without blame before him in love: 5 Having predestinated us unto the adoption of children by Jesus Christ to himself, according to the good pleasure of his will, 6 To the praise of the glory of his grace, wherein he hath made us accepted in the beloved.

1.4-6 Chosen us: God's searching desire for a people that would be one with Him brought about the possibility of a fallen man being declared holy and blameless. Believers are chosen by Him through the gospel first, (See Ps 65:42, John 15:16, Acts 2:39,40, Thess 2:13, 1 Pet 2:9,10) and did not love God first; He first loved mankind. (See 1 John 4:10, 1 John 4:19), The believers election results in a life of purpose and destiny that has been planned out in detail by God before the earth's foundation was ever laid. You are no accident.

In Him / In love: In Christ's prayer, recorded in John 17, he states that he was loved or "the beloved" before the foundation of the world. The child of God is "chosen in him in love" by virtue of spiritual **adoption**. As Israel was the "adopted sons of God" so is the Christian believer in Christ's love. Believers are beloved because Christ is first beloved.

Predestinated: The church (corporately) has a

pre-planned destiny that includes: full part in the inheritance that is only available to the family of God, and an identity as the "sons of God." This beautiful plan is available to whomsoever believeth in the Gospel of Jesus Christ (Rom 1:16) the only power that brings about salvation. No matter what kindred a person comes from, they all have access and acceptance in Christ when they believe and obey the Gospel. This membership into the family is made possible because it pleased God and was His intention from the beginning. Paul's life is an excellent example of God's predestined plan for man. (see Acts 9:11-15) When God's searching eye finds you, He'll put you in contact with a preacher that will instruct you in the way of salvation. As God did with Paul, so He does with all men.

Accepted in the beloved: The feeling of acceptance is one of the most wonderful feelings that a human being needs to live a joyous and fulfilling existence. A true believer is accepted by Christ; He or she does not accept Christ as their personal savior, but He accepts them. (See Eph 1:6, Acts 10:35, Rom 12:1,2, and 2 Cor 5:9) The teaching of "Accepting Christ as your personal savior" is totally refuted by true bible doctrine and cannot be found anywhere in the New Testament scriptures.

1.7 In whom we have redemption through his blood, the forgiveness of sins, according to the riches of his grace;

1.7 **Redemption**: is to ransom in full. A believer has a total deliverance from the slavery of sin and a full pardon from the sentence of death that sin requires.

(see John 8:34, Rom 7:14, Rom 6:16) In each of the previous mentioned scriptures, the word servant literally translates as slave. Through Christ's shed blood we have redemption from all the bonds of our former sin enslaved lives.

1.8 Wherein he hath abounded toward us in all wisdom and prudence;

1.8 God lavishes on us all manner of wisdom and insight when we reside in the wealth of His grace. A Christian not only has the privilege of knowing what the rest of the world doesn't know, but is also given the instructions and empowerment to act on that knowledge in his or her everyday life. God not only gives in abundance revelation to his chosen elect, but gives them practical insight on how to apply that knowledge in life.

1.9 Having made known unto us the mystery of his will, according to his good pleasure which he hath purposed in himself:

1.9 The knowledge that a believer has is knowledge that cannot be possessed by human efforts but has to obtained by God's disclosure (revelation). One has understanding of the **mysteries of God's will** because it is God's good pleasure to reveal them to him. The eunuch of Acts 8 had what was originally mystifying to him explained clearly by a God sent preacher named Phillip. Jesus is revealed to them that seek him. (Acts 8:28-35) The mysteries of God are clearly seen only through Jesus!

1.10 That in the dispensation of the fulness of times he might gather together in one all things in Christ,

both which are in heaven, and which are on earth; even in him:

1.10 To understand Jesus, one must be clear on the duality of His nature. He was all God manifest in the flesh (God rendered apparent, God shown and revealed tangibly 1 Tim 3:16). He was all man (Heb. 4:14-16). Through Jesus we have a representative of heaven and one of earth. In His right hand is all power in heaven and earth. In Jesus is all preeminence, both in the heavenly and the earthly realm. (Col. 1:18) Christ is the enabler for mankind to have the nature of the heavenly. That which once caused a man to be the enemy of God is buried with Christ. It is only in Christ that mankind can have new life, and be at peace with God.

1.11 In whom also we have obtained an inheritance, being predestinated according to the purpose of him who worketh all things after the counsel of his own will:

1.11 In Jesus we have Sonship and an inheritance from the beginning. A Key Point of Interest: in this text is the phrase: "...*worketh all thing after the counsel of his own will.*" We have a clear answer to the question often asked about (Gen 1:26) were it is written, "*And God said, Let us make man in our image, after our likeness:*" Gen 1:26 doesn't prove that God is separately existing in a plurality of persons but rather that He was creating man after the counsel of his own will.

1.12-14 That we should be to the praise of his glory, who first trusted in Christ. 13 In whom ye also trusted, after that ye heard the word of truth, the gospel of your salvation: in whom also after that ye believed, ye were

sealed with that holy Spirit of promise, 14 Which is the earnest of our inheritance until the redemption of the purchased possession, unto the praise of his glory.

1.12-14 We have become God's heritage and portion to live for the praise of His glory. To first the Jews, and then the Gentile have been preached the gospel and believed. Because of faith in the gospel of Jesus Christ, a believer is **sealed with that Holy Spirit of promise**. Believers of the gospel are sealed (*stamped, branded or marked*) with God's personal mark of possession and approval by way of the Spirit. The Holy Ghost is the down payment / guarantee (earnest) of our inheritance and it's just a foretaste of the wonderful reality of the world to come when all is one with God.

1.15-19 Wherefore I also, after I heard of your faith in the Lord Jesus, and love unto all the saints, 16 Cease not to give thanks for you, making mention of you in my prayers; 17 That the God of our Lord Jesus Christ, the Father of glory, may give unto you the spirit of wisdom and revelation in the knowledge of him: 18 The eyes of your understanding being enlightened; that ye may know what is the hope of his calling, and what the riches of the glory of his inheritance in the saints, 19 And what is the exceeding greatness of his power to us-ward who believe, according to the working of his mighty power,

1.15-19 Paul's prayer for the church was one of consistency and of thankfulness coupled with a desire for them to possess a disposition of wisdom and knowledge of Christ that would supersede their immediate and pressing circumstances. This understanding equips the church to know 1) what is the **Hope of your calling**: 2) riches of the glory of his inheritance 3) **His exceeding great power to us-ward**. To know the hope of your calling, is to understand the certainty of your success in pursuit of that calling.

1.20-23 Which he wrought in Christ, when he raised him from the dead, and set him at his own right hand in the heavenly places, 21 Far above all principality, and power, and might, and dominion, and every name that is named, not only in this world, but also in that which is to come: 22 And hath put all things under his feet, and gave him to be the head over all things to the church, 23 Which is his body, the fulness of him that filleth all in all.

1.20-23 In Christ is exerted all power and might (the very power to command death to give up the dead). His power is: unequalled and far above all other power. His rule and reign as Lord, is over all dominions. His name if for above every other name or title that can and will ever be given. (see Phil 2:9-11) Paul states that this is so, not only in this age, but also in the age and world to come.

Christ is over all power and authority in the church. His rule in the church is supreme because He is the head of it. In Christ Jesus the church is built, fits together (Eph 2:20, 1 Pet 2:6), and continues to grow (Isaiah 9:7) as God's holy temple (1 Cor 6:19). In Christ the Lord each individual believer is continually being built up as God's chosen dwelling place. Christ and the church are so "One" or unified, that Paul calls the church "His Body". Only in Jesus are we all complete! All that a believer can, or ever will need, is in Jesus.

Chapter 2

2.1-6

2.1 And you hath he quickened, who were dead in trespasses and sins;

2.1 Through Christ, the believer is "quickened" (made alive) from the death of his past life by the work of grace. This is one of the biggest reasons that Christians should be compassionate with them that are without Christ. One should never forget their life as a child of disobedience. Self-righteousness, unforgiveness and apathy are marks of one that has forgotten the miraculous resurrection that grace brought his or her way.

2.2 Wherein in time past ye walked according to the course of this world, according to the prince of the power of the air, the spirit that now worketh in the children of disobedience:

2.2 The "course of this world" (the ways, tendencies, thoughts, pursuits of the present evil age) were what the unbeliever's previous life consisted of. They didn't have control, but were caught up in the workings and dictates of the prince and power of air that always works in the children of disobedience.

2.3 Among whom also we all had our conversation in times past in the lusts of our flesh, fulfilling the desires of the flesh and of the mind; and were by nature the children of wrath, even as others.

2.3 "We all had" states the fact everyone, both Jew and Gentile believer alike, conducted themselves according to the course of the evilness of the present time. No one group could feel superior to another; because, all were sick with human nature and were "children of wrath" (people that are subject and deserving of God's judgment and punishment).

2.4-6 But God, who is rich in mercy, for his great love wherewith he loved us, 5 Even when we were dead in sins, hath quickened us together with Christ, (by grace ye are saved;) 6 And hath raised us up together, and made us sit together in heavenly places in Christ Jesus:

2.4-6 God, unwilling to leave sin-killed man in the grave of their damned existence, brought life to all man through His death, His burial and resurrection. To anyone that would be "In Him," (a powerful Pauline expression used 80 times in his letters and 10 times in Ephesians) is granted the honor and experience of sitting with Him in "heavenly places" (in His presence and into intimacy with Him). This privilege of sitting with Him in heavenly places isn't one that is a hope of the future, but rather is something that has already been made possible to the believer to live out in this present and evil day. It's God's way of giving his people a little taste of the world to come. This was all brought about because God is: rich in mercy (Eph 4), delighteth in mercy (Micah 7.18), forever enduring in mercy (Ps. 100.5, Ps. 103.17), and boundless in mercy (Ps. 108.4).

2.7-10 That in the ages to come he might shew the exceeding riches of his grace in his kindness toward us through Christ Jesus. 8 For by grace are ye saved through faith; and that not of yourselves: it is the gift of God: 9 Not of works, lest any man should boast. 10 For we are his workmanship, created in Christ Jesus unto good works, which God hath before ordained that we should walk in them.

2.7-10 "That he might shew" refers to God's purpose in what He did (4-6). It is to reveal to believers the true magnitude of His rich grace and kindness toward them. What is truly astonishing about this is that there is absolutely nothing about mankind that merits this type of divine affection. The fact that God really loves mankind, in spite of his fallen nature, is one of the things that makes grace so amazing. He is truly good and compassionate to us-ward (Rom 2.4). God's desire for man to know His grace and kindness caused Him to display His great workmanship through the church for the rest of the world to come and desire to experience this great salvation. It is not His will that anyone perish, but His compassionate desire is for all man to come to repentance (See Matt 9.13, Luke 5.32, 2 Pet 3.9). The gift of God's grace is what brings salvation. This means that no part of salvation is "of yourselves" or due to what we have done. One's salvation is God's gift to them. A man's salvation comes by grace but it is made real in his life through faith (trusting and believing in the atoning power of the blood of Jesus).

"Not of works" keeps man from thinking he'll reach heaven because he has earned the right of entrance there. Instead of man putting his works on display and receiving glory, God desires to get glory in the believer's life when the world sees him walking in the grip of His grace and favor. Jesus said, "ye are the light of the world" and that the world "may see your good works" but glorify the Father, which is in heaven (Matt 5:16). Though man's good works does not merit him his salvation experience, good works will always follow salvation.

2.11-22

2.11-13 Wherefore remember, that ye being in time past Gentiles in the flesh, who are called Uncircumcision by that which is called the Circumcision in the flesh made by hands; 12 That at that time ye were without Christ, being aliens from the commonwealth of Israel, and strangers from the covenants of promise, having no hope, and without God in the world: 13 But now in Christ Jesus ye who sometimes were far off are made nigh by the blood of Christ.

2.11-13 "Uncircumcision" was the way that Jews derogatorily referred to non-Jewish nationalities. This word sums up the great division that was present in that day. Citizenship in Israel afforded advantages, benefits, and privileges not afforded to non-citizens. Circumcision, the covenant sign of the Jew with God, set them apart from the rest of the world. The Gentile recipients of this letter did not have familial rights or covenant promises (those of Abraham, Isaac, Jacob, and David) in the family of God prior to becoming, (through faith) God's people. Now they have God's assistance and all the benefits of being one of God's chosen. They now were no more aliens but active participants in the culture of the family of God.

2.14-19 For he is our peace, who hath made both one, and hath broken down the middle wall of partition between us; 15 Having abolished in his flesh the enmity, even the law of commandments contained in ordinances; for to make in himself of twain one new man, so making peace; 16 And that he might reconcile both unto God in one body by the cross, having slain the enmity thereby: 17 And came and preached peace to you which were afar off, and to them that were nigh. 18 For through him we both have access by one Spirit unto the Father. 19 Now therefore ye are no more strangers and foreigners, but fellowcitizens with the saints, and of the household of God;

2.14-19 Jesus is our peace (Isa 9.6, Eph 2.14) He brought together what was always divided by his death on Calvary's cross. He destroyed the enmity (hatred) between the families of mankind and gave them a new family where they all were equal with each other as brothers and sisters in Christ. He abolished (rendered useless) the wall between the Jew and Gentile (the ceremonial law, not the moral law). All the specific dietary and cultural practices that had always kept the Jews from the Gentiles were no longer a reason to be separate. The disdain that each had for the other was done away with when Christ was crucified. From one man, Adam, came all nations of mankind, and through the second Adam (Jesus Christ) all nations are made one again. Through the cross came the ultimate plan of God; to bring all people back together as one family with the same name. Jesus is that family name. A believer takes on that name through the "circumcision not made with hands," water baptism in the name of Jesus Christ for the remission of sin. (See Col 2.11, Acts 2:38) This is the New Testament covenant sign with God. It is through this that believers are saved by grace through faith, and all nations are reconciled (made near to) God.

"Afar off" and "nigh" Jews had always had nearness to God through the temple but Gentiles were considered to be "far off," not only geographically, but also spiritually from the Lord God. Through the preaching of Jesus all are made near. Calvary not only brought the two nationalities together, but it brought them both to the Father by one Spirit. It is by that one Spirit that we all have admission into the family and access to our heavenly Father. The church is the family of God's household unified in Jesus Christ.

2.20-22 And are built upon the foundation of the apostles and prophets, Jesus Christ himself being the chief corner stone; 21 In whom all the building fitly framed together groweth unto an holy temple in the Lord: 22 In whom ye also are builded together for an habitation of God through the Spirit.

2.20-22 The church unified and is described here in a three-fold manner.
(1) "City:" having fellow citizenry (fellow citizens with the saints).
(2) "Family:" it unified as the (household of God).
(3) "Building/temple:" it is built on a foundation (teaching of the Apostles and Prophets) Jesus is it's "cornerstone". It's construction is Jesus centered and Jesus unified (held together).

Chapter 3

3.1 For this cause I Paul, the prisoner of Jesus Christ for you Gentiles,

3.1 Paul states that he is a prisoner (not of Rome) but of Jesus Christ. Everyone will have a prison-like experience in their life. Paul didn't allow his prison to prevent him from fulfilling the purpose of his calling. He knew that his present suffering would result in many that were "afar off" being brought nigh to God.

3.2 If ye have heard of the dispensation of the grace of God which is given me to you-ward:

3.2 "If ye have heard" is a statement implying that not all of the recipients of this letter had actually met Paul in person. This lends credence to the thought that this letter was most likely passed around throughout various different local churches in the manner of a circular letter.

From the word "Dispensation," derives our word economy. Dispensation here means: administration of, or stewardship of a household/estate; in the case of this passage, steward of the real currency of God's economy, grace. Paul was defining the nature of his Apostleship as a steward of the grace of God to the church.

3.3-7 How that by revelation he made known unto me the mystery; (as I wrote afore in few words, 4 Whereby, when ye read, ye may understand my knowledge in the mystery of Christ) 5 Which in other ages was not made known unto the sons of men, as it is now revealed unto his holy apostles and prophets by the Spirit; 6 That the Gentiles should be fellowheirs, and of the same body, and partakers of his promise in Christ by the gospel: 7 Whereof I was made a minister, according to the gift of the grace of God given unto me by the effectual working of his power.

3.3-7 The first and important part of Paul's revelation of the "mystery," was the revelation of who Jesus was (Acts 9). In addition to that was God's plan for the whole of mankind realized in the church / body of Christ. The church, not just meaning exclusively the Jew, but also to include the Gentile people. This line of thought would have never been considered by him prior to his Damascus road enlightenment. Paul alludes to the mystery in his writings that "in other ages sons of men" weren't permitted to see; that the Gentiles would be include as equals (fellow-heirs, of the same body, partakers of the promise of father Abraham) with the Jewish people (see Rom 11:25). Now that the knowledge was made known unto him, he was made a minister by the grace of God, to declare the explanation of this great mystery. v. 6 Spells out directly, that the Gentiles were: (1) "fellow heirs" meaning that they would enjoy an equal share in the heavenly inheritance, that they had no right to by virtue of their natural birth. (2) "of the same body" They were permitted an equal participation and standing in the family of god (Body of Christ). (3) "Partakers of his promise" The covenant that God made with Abraham. That promise (Abraham's) was and is received by faith (see Gal 3.18, Gal 3.25-29). Any that believe "In Christ" are fellow-heirs" and recipients of the promise of Abraham by faith in the gospel.

3.8-9 Unto me, who am less than the least of all saints, is this grace given, that I should preach among the Gentiles the unsearchable riches of Christ; 9 And to make all men see what is the fellowship of the mystery, which from the beginning of the world hath been hid in God, who created all things by Jesus Christ:

3.8-9 Paul's expression of great humility only further spread the message of the unsearchable rich's of Christ. He was vehemently opposing the church with threats, slaughter and warrants for the arrest of anyone who dared believe in this Jesus the Christ (see Acts 9.1,2). He, most likely, always remembered what great damage that he had done before he was stopped in his tracks by the blinding revelation of Jesus. Nothing makes anyone more humble that remembering just how far God has brought them. His statements like: "me, the least of all saints" "me, least of the apostles" "by the grace of God I am what I am" (see 1 Cor 15.9,10) and "sinners, of whom I am chief" (1 Tim 1.15). In other words, "If God can save me, He can save anyone!" The burden of the ministry is to make all men know what is the fellowship of the mystery.

Point of Interest: "Created all things by Jesus Christ" The revelation that Jesus is God is once again seen in this passage. Gen 1.1 states that God is the creator. If all things were created by Jesus Christ, He must be God.

3.10-13 To the intent that now unto the principalities and powers in heavenly places might be known by the church the manifold wisdom of God, 11 According to the eternal purpose which he purposed in Christ Jesus our Lord: 12 In whom we have boldness and access with confidence by the faith of him. 13 Wherefore I desire that ye faint not at my tribulations for you, which is your glory.

3.10-13 "Manifold" (many sided, intricate in variety, and countless in aspects) Not only is the church God's way of declaring His marvelous and multifaceted wisdom to mankind, it is His way of showing the authorities and rulers of the spiritual sphere, His unequalled genius. (See Eph 6.10-18) This has been God' purpose all along and is why that the church should have boldness and confident access in His presence. The church has limitless access to the innumerable aspects of God's unsearchable riches (their revelation of Jesus Christ). Paul desired for the church to have strength of heart because they should believe that his suffering was for their advantage and in their behalf.

3.14-19 For this cause I bow my knees unto the Father of our Lord Jesus Christ, 15 Of whom the whole family in heaven and earth is named, 16 That he would grant you, according to the riches of his glory, to be strengthened with might by his Spirit in the inner man; 17 That Christ may dwell in your hearts by faith; that ye, being rooted and grounded in love, 18 May be able to comprehend with all saints what is the breadth, and length, and depth, and height; 19 And to know the love of Christ, which passeth knowledge, that ye might be filled with all the fulness of God.

3.14-19 Paul's prayer for the Jesus named family of heaven and earth, was that they would understand their three-fold grant. (1) They'd be strengthened by the might of Christ's Spirit inwardly. Not only does the believer have a life that is "In Christ" but Christ actually lives in them by faith. This faith will result in a place of permanence for Christ to dwell in each believer's life. "Being rooted and grounded in love." "Rooted" is an agricultural term. The root system of a plant provides it's nourishment necessary for life and it's stability for growth. "Grounded" is an architectural term that implies foundational underlaying. A building is only as strong and secure as it's underlaying. Being rooted and grounded in God's love, is to know that you will always have the sustenance needed for life and growth as a "Tree of Righteousness" (see Ps 1.1-3, Isa 61.1-3), and the underlaying of stability necessary to building a life that will withstand the storms of life (see Eph 2.20,21). (2) "Comprehend the love of Christ" is to know that His love for you is not aptly described with spatial nouns such as "breadth," "length," "depth," and "height". Paul's vocabulary was inadequate to fully describe how far-reaching that the love of Christ really is. There is not enough space in the universe to contain the vocabulary that it would take to truly define the love that Jesus has for His church. One couldn't possibly know the extent of God's love for them. (3) "Filled with the fullness of God" is to experience for yourself this filling and flooding of Christ's love in your own life. Paul's most effective explanation was to pray that everyone would experience for themselves the love that had so radically changed his life. Oh taste and see that the Lord is good! (Ps 34.8)

3.20-21 Now unto him that is able to do exceeding abundantly above all that we ask or think, according to the power that worketh in us, 21 Unto him be glory in the church by Christ Jesus throughout all ages, world without end. Amen.

3.20-21 Whatever one's prayer is to God, He is willing and able to exceed "abundantly" in the granting of anything you could ever ask or think. This excess is of provision, for all of life's need, is readily available according to the power that is at work within the heart of a child of God.

Chapter 4

4.1-3 I therefore, the prisoner of the Lord, beseech you that ye walk worthy of the vocation wherewith ye are called, 2 With all lowliness and meekness, with longsuffering, forbearing one another in love; 3 Endeavouring to keep the unity of the Spirit in the bond of peace.

4.1-3 Earlier is this letter, Paul spelled out the wonders of Christ's love that the believer was blessed to live in. Here he shifts to exhorting them how to lead lives worthy and befitting of their divine calling. He stated again, as he did earlier (Eph 3.1), that he was the "prisoner of the Lord" and then told them that they should endeavor to keep unity in the "bond of peace." Bonds are for the purpose of binding but peace is liberating. The best hope that anyone has of living in the liberating rule and reign of the Prince of Peace is their attachment to the church (body of Christ). The three virtues listed here that enables the believer to walk worthy of their calling are: lowliness, meekness, and long-suffering. Once again, Paul was letting them know that it wasn't their goodness that produced a condition of worthiness. The believer's best hope at maintaining a walk worthy was to focus less on "Me" and more on "We". True peace is achieved when all are willing to limit their personal liberties for the good of the whole body of believers (See 1 Cor 10.23-33). If one ever realizes the fulfillment of his calling, he will have to say as John the Baptist said, "He must increase, but I must decrease" (see John 3.30).

4.4-6 There is one body, and one Spirit, even as ye are called in one hope of your calling; 5 One Lord, one faith, one baptism, 6 One God and Father of all, who is above all, and through all, and in you all.

4.4-6 This passage further illuminates the unity that the church has with God. "One body" -the body of Christ; the church, "one Spirit" -the one and same Spirit that gives life to all believers (2 Cor 3.17), "one hope" - the hope of an eternal home in heaven and access to the Father (Eph 2.18), "one Lord" - Jesus is Lord of all (Acts 2.36), "one faith" -only one doctrine and church (the Apostle's doctrine), "one baptism" - from Greek word (baptisma) meaning; to immerse, submerge, to make whelmed (fully wet) (see Acts 2.38, Acts 8.16, Acts 10.48, Acts 19.5, and Paul's testimony of his baptism Acts 22.16). "One God and Father" (see Duet 6.4). This one God is over all, through all, and in all.

4.7-10 But unto every one of us is given grace according to the measure of the gift of Christ. 8 Wherefore he saith, When he ascended up on high, he led captivity captive, and gave gifts unto men. 9 (Now that he ascended, what is it but that he also descended first into the lower parts of the earth? 10 He that descended is the same also that ascended up far above all heavens, that he might fill all things.)

4.7-10 Though there be diversity of spiritual gifts (see 1 Cor 12.4-14), not all in the church have the same gift. All spiritual gifts are given to edify the church not the individual believer. Everyone in the body of Christ is given the gift of grace (God's divine empowerment in the believer's life to do His will). "According to the measure of" It can be understood also that, the ministry is the gift of Christ. Not all ministers are the same and vary in abilities, but one should be thankful when there is a minster in their life that is an especially liberal dispenser of the wonderful grace of god (Eph 3.2) We are expected to minister in the church according to the measure of that gift (the news of God's unmerited favor) that has been entrusted to us (1 Pet 4.10). Each member has their own role to play in the body of Christ as each member does in the human body. "Led captivity captive" Paul references Ps 68.18 as an illustration of Christ bestowing spiritual gifts to His church. "He ascended up on high," describes God as a victorious warrior returning to Mt Zion and bringing back spoils of war to lavish on Israel (gave gifts unto men). This is also true of Christ and the church. Jesus came to earth for the purpose of mankind's redemption; then He returned to heaven having conquered Satan and his demonic forces (led captivity captive). He then gave "spiritual gifts" unto the church (the spoils of war), for her edification and growth.

4.11-16 And he gave some, apostles; and some, prophets; and some, evangelists; and some, pastors and teachers; 12 For the perfecting of the saints, for the work of the ministry, for the edifying of the body of Christ: 13 Till we all come in the unity of the faith, and of the knowledge of the Son of God, unto a perfect man, unto the measure of the stature

of the fulness of Christ: 14 That we henceforth be no more children, tossed to and fro, and carried about with every wind of doctrine, by the sleight of men, and cunning craftiness, whereby they lie in wait to deceive; 15 But speaking the truth in love, may grow up into him in all things, which is the head, even Christ: 16 From whom the whole body fitly joined together and compacted by that which every joint supplieth, according to the effectual working in the measure of every part, maketh increase of the body unto the edifying of itself in love.

4.11-16 This passage more specifically defines the church's essential ministerial gifts. The gift of the various ministries in the church were put there for her completion (to fully equip her), and to build up the church (body of Christ). Through the ministry, in the church, she develops into a body that is unified in oneness of faith (doctrine) and the full and accurate knowledge of Christ. The church grows up into, and matches up to "the standard of Christ" because of the ministerial gifts given to her. The gift of the ministry keeps the church from being tossed about and changing, (like a ship in a stormy sea), by the constantly changing fads and whims of popular generational trends. These whims are always motivated my devious and deceiving men that have their own personal agendas. The ministry should always build up the church, increase her knowledge of the Lord, and protect her from self-centered false prophet's whose motivations are personal gratification and love of money. True ministry is motivated by a sincere love for the church; and also, it's desire is for the body to grow up into Him which is the head. It is by and through Jesus that the church has it's being (Acts 17.28). Without Jesus, the church does not fit together and it does not adapt to meet its needs. The church walks together, works together, helps heal itself, and thoroughly functions because Christ placed these spiritual gifts in her.

4.17-21 This I say therefore, and testify in the Lord, that ye henceforth walk not as other Gentiles walk, in the vanity of their mind, 18 Having the understanding darkened, being alienated from the life of God through the ignorance that is in them, because of the blindness of their heart: 19 Who being past feeling have given themselves over unto lasciviousness, to work all uncleanness with greediness. 20 But ye have not so learned Christ; 21 If so be that ye have heard him, and have been taught by him, as the truth is in Jesus:

4.17-21 The Christian walk (life) is different than that of the world. The child of God's life is not empty and futile "vanity of their mind" but is one that is filled with purpose. Things are right, hearts are at peace, and there is joy in the Holy Ghost (Rom 14.17) when one's will is wholly submitted to God's. Many in the world are blind to, and alienated from, the ways of God simply because they refuse to see. The world is "past feeling" (become calloused toward a life in Christ) and have given themselves over to unrestrained sensuality. They are quick and eager to indulge in any form of impurity that their whims suggest. The believer has learned different if he really has heard about and been taught Jesus. The church lives clean lives because they live a life of the informed. The believer does live like the Lord because he is forced to; he lives in the ways of Christ because he knows to.

4.22-24 That ye put off concerning the former conversation the old man, which is corrupt according to the deceitful lusts; 23 And be renewed in the spirit of your mind; 24 And that ye put on the new man, which after God is created in righteousness and true holiness.

4.22-24 When one has been taught by Christ, they will make a complete lifestyle change (one that is no longer fooled into chasing every false illusion of fleshly fulfillment). Those that are students of the Lord Jesus are constantly thinking with a new and fresh mind (renewed in the spirit of your mind). The new life that results, is a witness to the world that God makes a totally new creature out of the Christian believer (2 Cor 5.17).

4.25-32 Wherefore putting away lying, speak every man truth with his neighbour: for we are members one of another. 26 Be ye angry, and sin not: let not the sun go down upon your wrath: 27 Neither give place to the devil. 28 Let him that stole steal no more: but rather let him labour, working with his hands the thing which is good, that he may have to give to him that needeth. 29 Let no corrupt communication proceed out of your mouth, but that which is good to the use of edifying, that it may minister grace unto the hearers. 30 And grieve not the holy Spirit of God, whereby ye are sealed unto the day of redemption. 31 Let all bitterness, and wrath, and anger, and clamour, and evil speaking, be put away from you, with all malice: 32 And be ye kind one to another, tenderhearted, forgiving one another, even as God for Christ's sake hath forgiven you.

4.25-32 This passage gives some practical evidence and ways that a believer can "put off" the old man and "put on" a new man's nature. The "new man" looks more and more like his heavenly Father. A true child of God will be honest, self-controlled, and quick to forgive. The new believer will be content with what the Lord has provided and consistently affecting those around him, in a positive fashion, by his lifestyle witness that reflects Jesus Christ.

Chapter 5

5.1-5 Be ye therefore followers of God, as dear children; 2 And walk in love, as Christ also hath loved us, and hath given himself for us an offering and a sacrifice to God for a sweetsmelling savour. 3 But fornication, and all uncleanness, or covetousness, let it not be once named among you, as becometh saints; 4 Neither filthiness, nor foolish talking, nor jesting, which are not convenient: but rather giving of thanks. 5 For this ye know, that no whoremonger, nor unclean person, nor covetous man, who is an idolater, hath any inheritance in the kingdom of Christ and of God.

5.1-5 When a believer begins the process of putting off the old man and putting on the new man, he must learn the way that a new man in Christ walks. "Followers of God" means to be an imitator of God. Like a child follows its parents and does what they see them do, a believer follows close behind the Lord hearing, reading, and loving His word and way. When one follows God as a child, they no longer allow the base and carnal desires of the flesh to reign in their life (see 1 Cor 6.9-11). It is certain that anyone practicing sexual vice, impurity of thought and life, has no part in the church or inheritance in the kingdom of God.

These types of practices are so unlike Christ that Paul was horrified at the thought of anyone in the church being identified as one continuing to do such things. A true child of God presents themselves daily as an offering of worship and praise to God by willingly submitting their human will and passions to God (see Rom 12.1,2). A believers' walk is one of morality (free from sexual vice). Not only does one's walk change; his talk changes too. His speech is no longer foolish and obscene like it used to be.

5.6-7 Let no man deceive you with vain words: for because of these things cometh the wrath of God upon the children of disobedience. 7 Be not ye therefore partakers with them.

5.6-7 Don't allow anyone to convince you that vain and filthy conversation is permissible. Don't join in with this type of unclean talk because it will surely bring down the wrath of God upon you. Paul was not saying, "Stay away from sinners." Rather, he was instructing us not to partner with or be sharers in their sin.

5.8-10 For ye were sometimes darkness, but now are ye light in the Lord: walk as children of light: 9 (For the fruit of the Spirit is in all goodness and righteousness and truth;) 10 Proving what is acceptable unto the Lord.

5.8-10 "Darkness" refers to the old life and it's traits. Before Christ, a person acted in ignorance not knowing what was pleasing or displeasing to the Lord. Now as "children of light" believers live like children that have loving and attentive parents who teach them how to conduct themselves along the way. One learns what pleases the Lord in the process of "becoming new" (see 2 Cor 5.17) and their lives are proof of what is acceptable to Him.

5.11-17 And have no fellowship with the unfruitful works of darkness, but rather reprove them. 12 For it is a shame even to speak of those things which are done of them in secret. 13 But all things that are reproved are made manifest by the light: for whatsoever doth make manifest is light. 14 Wherefore he saith, Awake thou that sleepest, and arise from the dead, and Christ shall give thee light. 15 See then that ye walk circumspectly, not as fools, but as wise, 16 Redeeming the time, because the days are evil. 17 Wherefore be ye not unwise, but understanding what the will of the Lord is.

5.11-17 To "reprove" is to (convict, tell a fault). Let your lives be as a contrast to expose and convict those that live and do the things of darkness. Do not participate with the world, but rather live your life as an example of light to the world. Light and darkness have no fellowship (see 2 Cor 6.14). The believer does not speak the same language or live the same lifestyle as they that walk in darkness because they have had the privilege of being taught better. It's not that they are better, but they have the light (knowledge of what is pleasing to God) in them to help them in their walk. Believers have a responsibility to walk the light of the Lord before the world (see Matt 5.16) and drive out the darkness around them. In this dark and evil day our light is becoming increasingly more effective. "Redeeming the time" Make the most of every opportunity that is afforded you. Buy up every chance that is offered to let His Light shine in the darkness of the world that is around you. The wise man stated in Prov. 4:18 that the walk of the righteous is like the breaking of the dawn that shines more and more until it reaches the full strength of day.

5.18-21 And be not drunk with wine, wherein is excess; but be filled with the Spirit; 19 Speaking to yourselves in psalms and hymns and spiritual songs, singing and making melody in your heart to the Lord; 20 Giving thanks always for all things unto God and the Father in the name of our Lord Jesus Christ; 21 Submitting yourselves one to another in the fear of God.

5.18-21 "Filled with the Spirit" When someone receives the gift of the Holy Ghost (scripturally evidenced by speaking with other tongues), they have Christ in them. The Christ in them (the Holy Ghost) is now what stimulates their lifestyle instead of what this world offers as stimulants to the body. The world's influences will always result in debauchery and death (see James 1.13-15). A Spirit filled life will be one that bears these following results: (1) Believers exhort and edify each other with songs, hymns and spiritual conversation. (2) They sing and make melodies to the Glory of God in their heart. (3) They are thankful for what God has done for them. (4) There is a mutual submission to God's will and to His people.

5.22-27 Wives, submit yourselves unto your own husbands, as unto the Lord. 23 For the husband is the head of the wife, even as Christ is the head of the church: and he is the saviour of the body. 24 Therefore as the church is subject unto Christ, so let the wives be to their own husbands in every thing. 25 Husbands, love your wives, even as Christ also loved

the church, and gave himself for it; 26 That he might sanctify and cleanse it with the washing of water by the word, 27 That he might present it to himself a glorious church, not having spot, or wrinkle, or any such thing; but that it should be holy and without blemish.

5.22-27 Christ's relationship with the church is described like a marriage between a man and a woman should be. Wives (the church) are to adapt themselves to their own husbands (Christ) as a service unto the Lord. The church's salvation is completely because Christ gave His life for her. The wife should be dependent upon, and submitted to, the husband that gives himself completely to her wellbeing. In "every thing" the husband is the head and he is to lead "in the fear of God." The wife is to be "subject to" (subordinate and obedient to) the husband in everything. Let us not forget that Eph 5.21 explicitly states that they are to be "submitted one to another" in the fear of God. Ultimately, the husband's disposition to his wife is to be one of sacrificial love, service, and protection.

5.28-33 So ought men to love their wives as their own bodies. He that loveth his wife loveth himself. 29 For no man ever yet hated his own flesh; but nourisheth and cherisheth it, even as the Lord the church: 30 For we are members of his body, of his flesh, and of his bones. 31 For this cause shall a man leave his father and mother, and shall be joined unto his wife, and they two shall be one flesh. 32 This is a great mystery: but I speak concerning Christ and the church. 33 Nevertheless let every one of you in particular so love his wife even as himself; and the wife see that she reverence her husband.

5.28-33 "As their own bodies" When God created the institution of marriage; He did so because it is not good for man to be alone. From Adam's rib, God fashioned the help-meet suitable for his specific needs (see Gen 2.18, 2.21-24). God did not use a bone from Adam's hand or foot, but He used one from his breast. This is why the husband cherishes the wife and doesn't walk all over her or abuse her. In this exhortation, Paul uses many more words to instruct the husband than he does the wife. The husband's conduct, will either help his wife or it will hinder her in being what God called her to be. There is no room in any marriage where one's interests ends and the other's begins. Selfishness is the antithesis of unity in both the church and in a marriage. The oneness of a Godly marriage will result in each spouse giving all of themselves to the other for their mutual benefit.

Chapter 6

6.1-4 Children, obey your parents in the Lord: for this is right. 2 Honour thy father and mother; which is the first commandment with promise; 3 That it may be well with thee, and thou mayest live long on the earth. 4 And, ye fathers, provoke not your children to wrath: but bring them up in the nurture and admonition of the Lord.

6.1-4 We are to live submitted in our home life, in our worship life, and in our everyday life outside the church while amongst the world (see 5.22,23). Children are to obey and honor their parents, especially them that are in the Lord. This is the fifth of what is called the Ten Commandments (Ex 20.3-17). "Honor" means much more than just obey. It's to show all due reverence to them (hold them in high esteem). This was the first commandment with promise attached to it. The promise in this commandment was that there would be a long life for those that obeyed it by honoring their parents. God's desire for obedience is beautifully spelled out by Isaiah where he wrote, "If ye be willing and obedient, ye shall eat the good of the land" (Isa 1.19) If one is both willing and obedient they will have plenty. If children obey and honor their parents in the

Lord, they will be blessed with plenty of life. "Provoke Not" Fathers are to instruct and raise their children justly, not provoking (not being unduly severe, losing their temper, being cruel, sarcastic and humiliating, or misusing authority and being abusive). "Nurture" is to train, to tutor, to instruct with discipline one's children with emphasis on teaching them in the ways of the Lord.

6.5-9 Servants, be obedient to them that are your masters according to the flesh, with fear and trembling, in singleness of your heart, as unto Christ; 6 Not with eyeservice, as menpleasers; but as the servants of Christ, doing the will of God from the heart; 7 With good will doing service, as to the Lord, and not to men: 8 Knowing that whatsoever good thing any man doeth, the same shall he receive of the Lord, whether he be bond or free. 9 And, ye masters, do the same things unto them, forbearing threatening: knowing that your Master also is in heaven; neither is there respect of persons with him.

6.5-9 Give care and concern to how you go about doing your job as your employer wishes (knowing it is the Lord that gave you the employment in the first place). "Men pleasers" a true child of God does what is right even when men are not watching because it is in their heart and they know that God is watching. With "Good will" is to always act in the best interests of them that employ you. One's conduct on earth is a visible reflection of their inward knowledge that all that they do will ultimately be rewarded accordingly by the Lord (the One that all our life's work is for). "Ye Masters" If you are blessed to have a business, always deal justly with them that you employ. Don't handle employees with partiality. God is impartial (2 Chron 19.7, Prov 24.23, Prov 28.21, Rom 2.11, Col 3.25, 1 Pet 1.17).

6.10-13 Finally, my brethren, be strong in the Lord, and in the power of his might. 11 Put on the whole armour of God, that ye may be able to stand against the wiles of the devil. 12 For we wrestle not against flesh and blood, but against principalities, against powers, against the rulers of the darkness of this world, against spiritual wickedness in high places. 13 Wherefore take unto you the whole armour of God, that ye may be able to withstand in the evil day, and having done all, to stand.

6.10-13 In conclusion, Paul reminds the church that our strength is in the Lord. We are empowered through our union and connection with Christ. Believers are provided armor to protect and help them to stand in this warfare that is waged against them by the carefully devised schemes and tactics of the devil. "Wrestle" is to combat in a close and personal fashion. War against Satan is fought in a "hand to hand combat" style (it's personal). We are not fighting humanity. We fight "principalities" (rulers seen and unseen), "powers" (authorities seen and unseen), "Rulers" (world rulers), and "Spiritual wickedness" (wicked spiritual beings, fallen angels, demons and even Lucifer himself. If the church will survive and be victorious, it must put on the whole armor of God. We face a formidable foe that we can only defeat through the strength and power of the Lord. "Done all" Having donned the armor of the Lord, the believer is able to resist and stand his ground in the evil day of danger, and is firmly braced for Satan's certain future attacks.

6.14-17 Stand therefore, having your loins girt about with truth, and having on the breastplate of righteousness; 15 And your feet shod with the preparation of the gospel of peace; 16 Above all, taking the shield of faith, wherewith ye shall be able to quench all the fiery darts of the wicked. 17 And take the helmet of salvation, and the sword of the Spirit, which is the word of God:

6.14-17 The "armor of God" consists of six pieces. (1) "Girdle of Truth" keeps all of the armor together for effective and fierce fighting like the battle girdle of ancient soldiers did. The enemy does not use brute force in his attacks; he is subtle in his tactics and devices. The knowledge of the truth is the only way that a Christian soldier can fight all the lies and devious ways of the devil. (2) "Breastplate of Righteousness" This alludes to Isaiah's prophetic depiction of Christ our Savior (Is 59.17). The breastplate of righteousness represents holy character and moral conduct that guards and keeps the heart (Prov 4.23). With this piece of armor on we truly are followers (imitators of) Jesus Christ (Eph 5.1). (3) "Gospel Shoes" We carry the good news of Jesus (Prince of Peace Is 9.6). For this gospel message to be effective, it must be carried in a righteous way. The message of the gospel is first pure (truth) and it is peaceable (Jam 3.17). Isaiah stated that the work of righteousness shall be peace and it's effects would be quietness and assurance forever in peaceable habitations (Is 32.17,18). (4) "Shield of Faith" Most importantly, remember that our strength and might in this battle is in the Lord. Always take God at His word and Satan will not be successful in piercing you through with his fiery darts of doubt. We may at times learn of the Lord with questions, but one must never make the fatal mistake of doubting Him. The enemy always attacks the believer by questioning the reliability of God's word. Protect yourself and fight the devils onslaughts like Christ did in the wilderness (Mat 4.1-11). The "It is written" defense will put out every one of the devil's fiery darts of doubt. (5) "Helmet of Salvation" Our assurance of salvation is our hope (1 Thess 5.8). Our final end is certain in Christ (Jer 29.11). When fighting for the Lord, we are certain of victory in the end. (6) "Sword of the Spirit" When a believer speaks the word of God, there is great victorious power. Speak the scripture to the adversary and you will be more than a conqueror in Christ (Rom 8.37-39).

6.18-24 Praying always with all prayer and supplication in the Spirit, and watching thereunto with all perseverance and supplication for all saints; 19 And for me, that utterance may be given unto me, that I may open my mouth boldly, to make known the mystery of the gospel, 20 For which I am an ambassador in bonds: that therein I may speak boldly, as I ought to speak. 21 But that ye also may know my affairs, and how I do, Tychicus, a beloved brother and faithful minister in the Lord, shall make known to you all things: 22 Whom I have sent unto you for the same purpose, that ye might know our affairs, and that he might comfort your hearts. 23 Peace be to the brethren, and love with faith, from God the Father and the Lord Jesus Christ. 24 Grace be with all them that love our Lord Jesus Christ in sincerity. Amen.

6.18-24 Paul connects prayer with standing and withstanding in this spiritual fight. He instructs the church to pray continually, especially when attacked by the enemy. Without the Spirit's help and direction (acquired in prayer), the armor of God is of little to no effect (Rom 8.26). We all have access to our heavenly Father by that one Spirit and it (the Spirit) cries out to Him for help in times of distress (Eph 2.18, Rom 8.15, Gal 4.6). Each one must have a personal prayer life, and the church's survival is dependent upon perseverance in corporate prayer. Paul instructs the church to pray for believers everywhere and asks that they pray for him that God would give him liberty to speak boldly and courageously the mystery of the gospel. He explains that he sent beloved Tychicus with this letter to let them know how he (Paul) was doing, and to also bring to them comfort, encouragement, consolation, and strength of heart.

www.ingramcontent.com/pod-product-compliance
Lightning Source LLC
Chambersburg PA
CBHW040418100526
44588CB00022B/2864